Easter Vigil

Easter Vigil

Poems by Ann Neelon

1995 Anhinga Prize for Poetry
Selected by Joy Harjo

Anhinga Press
Tallahassee, Florida

Library of Congress Card Catalog Number: 96-083909
ISBN: 0-938078-44-5

Printed in the United States of America

Cover art and design by Lynne Knight
Book design and production by Geoffrey Brock

*This publication is sponsored in part by a grant from the
Florida Department of State, Division of Cultural Affairs,
and the Florida Arts Council.*

Anhinga Press is a nonprofit corporation dedicated wholly
to the publication and appreciation of fine poetry.

ANHINGA PRESS
P.O. Box 10595
Tallahassee FL 32302

ACKNOWLEDGMENTS

Grateful acknowledgment is made to the following publications in which the following poems previously appeared: *Calyx*: San Juan del Río Coco; To a Human Fetus in a Jar, Seen in the Offices of COLPROSUMAH, a Union of 27,000 Honduran Teachers. *The Gettysburg Review*: World Series. *Ironwood*: Today at Marché Sandaga. *Manoa*: Grandfather's Peonies; Night Owl; Pale Moon Over Kigali. *The Massachusetts Review*: Whatever Crept Away. *The Mississippi Valley Review*: Palmerola Air Force Base; Peace Mission: Visit to Patio Grande, a Coffee-Growing Cooperative. *Nebraska English Journal*: Oh Earth. *Open Places*: Old Cronies. *Pequod*: Tree of an Emigré. *Sequoia*: Argument from the Heart. *The Stanford Weekly*: The Nun Story. "World Series" was reprinted in the anthology *Diamonds Are A Girl's Best Friend: Women Writers on Baseball*, edited by Elinor Nauen, Faber and Faber, 1994.

I wish to thank the Corporation of Yaddo, the Arts Council of Santa Clara County, Stanford University and the Kentucky Foundation for Women for fellowships which enabled me to complete this work.

Thanks also to all my teachers, particularly those of the Stanford workshops: Simone DiPiero, Ken Fields and Denise Levertov, with special thanks to Denise for teaching me that being an artist means believing in a vision.

I also wish to thank Squire Babcock, Jay Klokker, Mary Koncel, Dennis Leder, S. J., Nancy McCrickard, Fran Quinn, Ben Sáenz and Margaret Szumowski for their astute comments on poems and for conversations that have kept me alive as an artist.

Finally, I wish to thank my brothers and sisters (Kathleen Cadigan, William Neelon, Maureen Neelon, John Neelon, Ellen Neelon and Beth Neelon) and my husband and son (Richard Parker and Liam Parker) for living through these poems with me.

For my mother,
Evelyn Rose Neelon,
and in memory of my father,
William Raphael Neelon
(1926—1976).

TABLE OF CONTENTS

I.

II.

III.

IV.

The tombs of all those
who have loved their fellow
human beings are empty.

–*The Gospel in Solentiname*

I

OLD CRONIES

When a man dies, we, the bereaved ones,
sit in his kitchen and tell jokes
to give his soul enough ballast to fly home.

While he makes progress, we regress.
We open his encyclopedia of ailments and laugh
about his chronic indigestion,
about his lifelong fear of botulism.
We tell stories his grown children have never heard:
how he lined his mother's Victory Garden with sauerkraut,
how the stench won the War.

We talk with our mouths full, for we are trying
to take in as much as he did in a lifetime,
we are stuffing ourselves with loss.
The hams, the turkeys, the cranberry breads, are the gifts
of the neighbors, who pay tribute to the dead man's
eccentricities of appetite.

When we have drunk enough of the dead man's liquor
to experience the giddiness of flight, his widow
makes us eat more, for the giddiness of flight
must belong only to her husband.

The world is full of men she could have married.
We are a few specimens. We are a few
artichoke hearts in olive oil.

One by one, we make our excuses. We gather
at the streetcorner, out of earshot, where we can watch
the wife of our dead friend lingering
over our dirty dishes as if she were lingering
over his last act of love, as if she could not set her feet
on the floor of grief after a night of so much ecstasy.

GRANDFATHER'S PEONIES

At 93, Grandfather is pretty wobbly.
He stoops like *homo erectus.*
Katelyn and Lauren are wobbly too, having just learned how to
      walk upright
to search for beauty in the indomitable way of their species.
Katelyn races out. She is afraid of Grandfather
—her great grandfather—
because he stares at her too raptly,
like an ape at a god.
Lauren stares back, admitting the ape in all of us,
our uncombed sorrow.

"It should have been me, it should have been me,"
Grandfather cried when Father died, hurtling himself away from us
like an insane man
into an invisible train.

Peonies blossom
on Grandfather's cheeks in the too-hot room.
Grandfather is in love with his nurse,
whose name is Carol.
She is strawberry blond.
"It's tough to be old, it's tough to be old,"
Grandfather complains brightly whenever she's around.
After every bath, there must be tea with Carol.
All week, Grandfather hoards sweets in tinfoil.
Carol never tells him that the date-nut bread is stale.
She is always grateful.

Grandfather used to give us peonies in wet napkins and tinfoil.
On the way home, we always sounded out the sign
to keep Mother happy—*IF YOU LIVED HERE,
YOU'D BE HOME NOW*—then we'd bury our faces again
in Grandfather's peonies. The meteor
of the city of Boston streaked by us:
gorgeous, gorgeous, gorgeous, gorgeous.

Father carried us, asleep with our mouths open, into the dark house.
Mother put the peonies in water.

"Ain't she pretty? Ain't she sweet?"
We did our best to cheer up Mother
when Grandfather sold his house and took up with a woman
        with bad grammar.
Grandmother hadn't been dead even a year.
Our memory of Grandmother was like the pearl
John had pushed up his nose once while Grandmother was
        babysitting.
It stuck and stuck.
We couldn't get it out of our nostrils.
Maybe we'd die from ingesting its beauty.
How had Grandfather forgotten?

Grandfather never told us the whole story,
but we knew his sweetheart had taken him for all his money
because of the anxiousness in his eyes.
Come on, Madame!
Come on, Madame!
Grandfather used to honk and honk
until we almost grew deaf
from his fear of driving home in the dark,
and Grandmother would say, "He's apopleptic. Good-bye, good-bye."
Grandfather had become his exasperating self again.
We took him in.

The other day at dinner, Grandfather
leapt up suddenly, as if he were 40 years old again and the leviathan
of the Depression were about to crush him.
Instead of cursing Hoover, he cursed me:
"Why can't you be a normal woman?
Why can't you get married and have children?"
then collapsed to his seat and attacked
his corn chowder like the last hobo in a soup line.

I had a hard time forgiving Grandfather
for condemning me for what the gods had not granted.

Every morning, Grandfather sweeps our kitchen.
His sweeping is like excruciatingly slow waltzing,
one two three, one two three,
trying not to get dizzy.
Sometimes he sweeps the dirt over our feet
without realizing it.
We have learned not to take the broom out of his hand.

A broom is a skinny woman.
Grandmother was round, with thick legs, like a table
upon which Grandfather was not afraid to place
everything he loved:
his two sons,
his two daughters,
his fifteen grandchildren.

Ashes to ashes, dust to dust, but the ashes and dust
are the petals we scatter in the wind.

Katelyn does not watch where she is going.
She runs right into Grandfather, her nemesis.
"Whoa," he says, "whoa," as he tries to regain his balance.
Katelyn runs to her mother.
Grandfather is a radiant monster.
She can almost see through his skin.

I am a little girl in a fast car fighting off sleep again.
I must not let Grandfather's peonies slip out of my hands.
My fingers open, open, although I try to close them.

THE NUN STORY

There were nuns in every branch of our family.
I imagined crows in black habits cawing
in the effulgence of my grandfather's crabapple blossoms,
crows with eyes like the seeds of crabapples.

When my uncles died young of heart attacks,
the nuns alone were undaunted.
They rushed onto the stage of grief
and knelt down like child actors, who knew
they were good at playing stumps in a haunted forest.
We prayed the rosary that night with the fervor
of wild animals.

Missionary nuns looked like doves not crows.
Sister Alphonsine who lived
in Sri Lanka, "the resplendent land," sent us postcards
of purple-faced monkeys called *langurs*
who reminded her of Our Lord's passion and death.
I looked into the solemn eyes of those monkeys
who were gluttons for hibiscus flowers
and I couldn't find any crown of thorns.

My grandmother was the nemesis of every nun.
Every spring she looked up at the crabapple blossoms
and remembered that on her Confirmation Day her arms
had been wrapped in rags not lace.
That is what one nun did to poor children,
who couldn't afford long-sleeved white dresses.

That is why so many heads turned at my brother's wedding,
when my uncles asked the nuns to dance.
My father, who was drunk too, rushed over to make amends,
but before he could reach their table,
the nuns had stormed out of the dance hall.
My father proposed a toast to their guardian angels.

ARGUMENT FROM THE HEART

I cannot take you into my arms,
here where so many rumors have started,
where so many salt shakers have unleashed winter storms.

So much salt has already been rubbed into this room,
into discussions, into blue fish,
into the stigmata of my three maiden aunts.

How can I hear your beating heart, when the men
in my family, the shirt-tailed drummers, are pounding
on the table in the ardor of their deprivation?

The table is groaning with another leaf,
and the grandchildren are hiding underneath,
teaching dolls their sexual alphabets.

And how can I insist on the tremulousness of your body,
when the humming of mouths is already this loud, when the
            love birds
are nesting in my uncles' hairy ears?

My spinal cord reverberates like the wineglasses
on my mother's table and my father,
the maestro, toasts to my desire.

My married sisters, who are unimpressed with love, begin
exchanging recipes for floods, for fires, for earthquakes
to make the teeth of bachelors chatter.

Our neighbors of a thousand years drop by with watermelons
the size of boulders that have taken over their gardens,
enough cargo to slake a festival of thirst.

And how can I take you into my arms, when my lips are already
            saturated
with pink flesh, when I am already spitting out seeds,
when for an inconceivable moment I have given up thirsting for you?

CRAZY-QUILT LOVE POEM,
FROM CALIFORNIA AND KENTUCKY

for Richard

The body is the shadow of the shadow
of the shadow of the heart.

You quoted Rumi, and I read
voraciously between the lines:
he loves me.

He loves me!
What an insane trembling.
We had barely survived the earthquake when we met.
I had run for my life out of a California building.
In hindsight, I see the plaster
falling from the ceiling
like the old-maid snows of yesteryear.

"Marriage is like a garden,"
the pre-Canaa counselor said. "You must water it
every day." I swore his advice
was hokey pokey until I touched my cheek
in a dark theatre during *Three Coins in a Fountain* and it was wet
with gratitude, WITH GRATITUDE,
because I was watching a love story and I wasn't lovelorn.
Palo Alto was not Rome.
The drought had turned the fountain
in front of the Post Office,
entitled *The Flame*,
into an egregious claw.
But the flames of my heart still burst out in watery streams.
You were waiting to kiss me under the marquee.
Your lips were my Tivoli.

True, being married can be awfully mundane.
Sometimes, over breakfast, we discuss

impending storms
as if we were strangers at a busstop.
Winter in Kentucky was grey and long.
Until spring came, we couldn't have singled out the catalpa tree
from the other trees in our backyard.
But then we noticed the huge-heartedness of each leaf.
But then we noticed the good grenade
of each blossom exploding
on what we would have guessed was a lousy day.
Oh joy, joy, joy, joy!

It's summer now, and we've planted a garden
for the first time in our lives.
We didn't want to be too ambitious.
Our garden plot
is the size of a prayer mat.
Yesterday, you got down on your knees
to plant okra seeds, which had swollen into black opals
overnight in a glass of tap water.
I held a seed too close to my eye.
It became the dark archway through which I saw we must pass
into the purest light.
The body is the shadow of the shadow of the shadow of the heart.

On our wedding day,
how tremblingly our hearts spoke.
Today, there will be no quaking in my bouquet
as I speak my heart.
I will love you jazzily in the jasmine.
I will love you foxily in the foxglove.
I will love you daffily in the daffodils.
I will love you rosily in the rosebed
all the days of my life.

OH EARTH

Earth Day, April 22, 1990

Oh earth, I'm embarrassing you with my grief again, tears
    streaming down my cheeks
like the rain in the rain forest where I have never been.
It is true, the other day I attended a concert where
    ethnomusicologists in bird masks
blew ancient whistles into the dense vegetation of the audience,
but afterwards, we did not need machetes to hack our way to
    the exits.
There were no orchids in star clusters shining with dew at our feet.
And if the darkness became a leafy cathedral in which we lost
    ourselves,
we found ourselves much too quickly when the lights came on.

It's not that I never want to go to Brazil,
but as a matter of inflexible policy I will not defect to a foreign
    country
in spring, when the California poppies cup themselves in the
    sunshine like begging bowls,
and I too, a trembling offering in the hands of the holy ones,
    grow humble enough, one afternoon, to be exalted.
There is a bridge over one of your streams, and I race toward it
    with the playmates of my second childhood.
We take turns playing the troll in *The Billygoats Gruff—Who's
that walking across my bridge?*—until,
oh earth, one of us slips, and we discover the salamanders
    mating in the stream.
We get our pants wet wading in for a better look. Suddenly, the
    sky opens up.
Hailstones pound apples into our cheeks. We take cold, but we
    warm up again in an old barn that smells like horses.

Oh earth, I know I won't live forever. The other day, picking
     blackberries
along an estuary, I cried out to the egrets in the tide pools, *This one*
     is sweet, this one
is even sweeter. I understood that sweetness does not last.
But when I heard a huge roar, I raced through stinging nettles
     to the sea
because I believe in eternity too, and, oh earth, may I never again
take eternity for granted, as you rush toward me, wave upon
     wave upon wave.

II

TREE OF AN EMIGRE

Still like a traveler, he sifts through the land, getting to know
      the trees first.
What's this, what's that—pine? eucalyptus? —in the language of
      infant fingers.
He lives on a block. His neighbor the young American once
      traveled to Russia on business.
When he got home, he said to the Russian émigré, "your trees
      are like our trees, your winters not much different."
The old man had spent years in the tundra, years abroad. His
      tongue was so thick with bark he couldn't answer.
Vinnitsa. Vladivostock. He lives outside now. He's getting wet.
Deep in the lung of tree, he lets the rain in. His children get
      dizzy running around him.
They sink in his shade, in the crisp apple umbra of flesh. Birds
      land. The man's arms warble.
Tree of his loneliness, tree of his loveliness. Tree, tree, tree.

TODAY AT MARCHE SANDAGA

Today I am braver than Mamadou Bamba.
I'm ready to juggle cabbages and teach everyone my real name.
Then I'll go woo all the vegetable ladies for carrots and mint
and flatter the fishmongers into giving me *tiof*.
I feel so strong today I may even throw stones
at the *bana-bana* men.

Look, today the market brats are thumping out my entrance on
    upside-down tomato cans.
They know I'm fierce enough for warpaint and tam-tams.
Oh bless them, the little thieves have stopped picking my pockets!

The little girls have all forgotten how to hiss.
How generous they are, roasting peanuts for their mothers
and picking flies from babies' eyes.
The cashews they sell taste like apples.
I am so courageous today
I may let them plant cornrows in my hair and pierce my ears.

What, have I grown a beard today or memorized
the Koran in my sleep?
The old men keep biting into hard bread
and recommending me gustily to Allah.
Today they expect me to answer important questions
about the nature of the universe and the circumferences of circles.
I drink strong coffee and put my feet up on rotting banana crates.
I spit tobacco,
then chew on a weed to clean my teeth.
How peaceful it is
sleeping under these black umbrellas!

Those cunning mounds of flesh, the lettuce ladies, are already
smacking their lips but I am too quick for them.
No more squished tomatoes!
Today I insist on fresh okra and live shrimp.

And for heaven's sake, no more rotten eggs!
I am so angry about the past that I tumble
all their eggshell pyramids and make puddles
of dead chickens.
Now they're afraid to make fun of my husband.
I tell them he kills elephants and keeps me happy all day long.

Oh, the marvelous cuts of meat I will buy today:
ribs dripping with blood, glistening sausages,
bone marrow fit for teething lions.
No more oxen fed on sawdust.
I have been hunting so long today I am really hungry.

And who are all these second wives clustering around the onion men?
Away, away, bickering women!
Can't you see Machmou and Abdoulaye
are taking you in with a grain of salt today?
I can read the palm of every bay leaf.
Do you think they'll make *me* pay for garlic?

CHICKEN TIED UP WITH A RED HANDKERCHIEF

Out of her good heart, my neighbor
gave me a chicken.
I was a stranger,
carnivorous. I had the knife
and the mind and the heart
to butcher that chicken in my yard.

The yard wasn't really my yard.
It belonged to Mame Diaga, my neighbor,
who said, "There is the river, the heart
you will drink"; who tied up the chicken
and sharpened the knife
and handed the knife to the stranger.

Now nothing was stranger
than standing in my own yard
and whispering, "Whose knife?"
Eyes on my neighbor,
I said to myself, "This chicken
will mock me if I lose heart."

Then Mame Diaga cupped me in his heart-
shaped hands like Allah, blue stranger.
It's not easy to fool a chicken
early in the morning in the chicken yard,
and I winced in the light at my neighbor
watching me flatter the tongue of my knife.

So, in the patient sun, the knife
glistened, and the pet escaped through the heart-
colored hole in the handkerchief owned by a neighbor.
Now I was a suffering, speechless stranger,
and if every plot I stepped into was a chicken yard,
how could I pick out my own bad chicken?

Now Mame Diaga said, "There is a chicken,
under the moon, fearing a knife
from someone else's yard."
So, under the spell of the chicken's moon, I set out, heart
nearly broken, ignorant of maps, following a stranger
with swollen legs, who trusted the luck of a neighbor.

When this chicken walks by the moon, my heart
flutters open like a summer yard. I yell, "Stranger, stranger,
eons ago my knife flew away. We grow old together, my
        sweetheart, my neighbor."

OMAK, WALKING WITH NANCY

Sagebrush the color of tin
in the fading winter light, quail
on the wing, and,
across the river from Saint Mary's
Indian Mission,
the matrices of orchards.

We walk to the waterfall in the canyon.
The snow-covered ground
is the wall of a cave
against which the shadows
of deer flicker.
We too can become invisible, disappear
into the blond grasses.

TO A HUMAN FETUS IN A JAR,
SEEN IN THE OFFICES OF COLPROSUMAH,
A UNION OF 27,000 HONDURAN TEACHERS

You are luminous,
you are luminous,
you are luminous,
in formaldehyde, anonymous
amber, like a photograph
of close relatives,
left behind in an attic.
Your skin looks soft.
The Madonna of Decaying Magnolias
wants to hold you in her fathomless lap.
You are the Christ Child
in the Christmas card the world sends
to the children
without pencils,
without teachers,
without schools.
Experience will teach them
in retrospect
how to read the handwriting
on the walls of their mothers' wombs.
Juan Ambrosio Sabio
will forgive me for half listening
to his statistics
about the lucky ones who will live long enough
to learn simple arithmetic:
two and two atrocities
equal a lifetime.
You are alive in me as the student
whose name
I can never remember,
the quiet one, whose sadness
I have been afraid to investigate.
You are my patient teacher.
I bow my head,
as you do,
waiting to be born.

PALMEROLA AIR FORCE BASE

We were not allowed to take pictures
of the camouflaged sandbags.
As my grandmother used to say, "My weight
is a military secret."
The sun was hot.
"In Honduras, Americans
walk on water," the lieutenant said,
welcoming us into the briefing room.
He took pride in the silhouettes of soldiers
in the margins of the white poster.
Nicaragua, 75,000;
El Salvador, 49,000;
Guatemala, 43,000.
On the blackboard: *Falcon's Eye*,
Big Pine, Crown Dragonfly.
Natural history as a euphemism
for counterinsurgency training.
"They menstruate, defecate, throw garbage, bathe
in the same water," the lieutenant said.
"We teach them how to go to the bathroom."
The day before, an activist in the Campesino Union
had insisted we go to Copan.
"There," he said, "the Mayans offer rose petals, candles,
incense wrapped in corn leaves.
Whoever offers the gifts
prays out loud and makes gestures
to arrest God's attention."
The lieutenant kept talking.
I could not get the smell of roses
out of the room.

SAN JUAN DEL RIO COCO

for *Esperanza Tórrez de Rivera*
Nicaragua, July 1987

The river is an exaggeration of a stream.
Here, a sorry horse snorts, humility
is taken for granted.

I am the country doctor
who cannot inoculate against hunger,
who removes a stethoscope
from her black bag and detects in these mountains
the beating heart of the world.

It is the rainy season, and my yellow boots
are an inspiration.
Even old men try them on,
insisting toothlessly on canaries.

Mothers shoo away their children,
who fly to me.
Today I am the flypaper,
hanging luminous in every doorway.
My body gets stickier and stickier in the heat.

At dusk, I cross town in a chorus of frogs.
Pastor González, who is not a priest
but can give out
the Holy Eucharist,
invites me into his home.
The electricity goes out, and we light candles.

It is difficult
to hear the mortars in the distance
over the cacophony of chickens.

Esperanza waits up for me
with her four daughters.
It is very late,
but she makes coffee with too much sugar.

At first I do not understand
that no one
in this sleepy town will sleep tonight.

PEACE MISSION: VISIT TO PATIO GRANDE, A COFFEE-GROWING COOPERATIVE

Nicaragua, 1987

We tell each other we would not make this trip
with anyone who was *not* afraid.
Twenty-four of us stand for 30 kilometers in an open *transporte*:
sticks of dynamite—we refuse to say this aloud—
waiting to be lit.

Or perhaps we are the *good* thieves from *Norteamérica*
and we are already luxuriating in Paradise.
No one will ambush angels and saints. Let's stop!
After the rain, leaves shimmer on the trees.
Besides, I have never held a coffee berry in my hand
or eaten a banana I picked myself!

Adelia, who stood guard last night in the trench around the
    houses,
greets us with circles under her eyes.
The worst part is the mosquitoes, she tells us, and holds out her
    hand that is like a relief map
of the mountains we have just driven across.

Children scramble up into the bombed truck
and wave at us enthusiastically, but from a distance,
like entertainers in a parade.
Their shyness lasts five minutes, enough time for Adelia
to give us the details of the attack: it was in broad daylight.
Four died and eleven were wounded running up the hill from
    the school.

Valvita's daughter is weak from giving birth.
Otherwise, the entire population of Patio Grande accompanies
    us to the four white crosses.

One is for the 19-year-old student teacher who came out to
      Patio Grande from Managua.
"We couldn't get anyone else," a man explains. "We don't even
      have blackboards."
Two are for women and the other for a six-year-old girl.

The *new* young teacher stops teaching to give us a tour of the
      bombed school.
"*Silencio*," he bellows at his students, but they chatter in the
      background like relentless birds.
Chouteau Chapin, a 77-year-old actress from the United States,
      has promised them a puppet show
about Zacchias, the man who climbed a tree to see Jesus.
As a dramatic opening, she orders me, a lowly stagehand, to
      make the leaves of the tree rustle.

Finally, it is time for lunch. While Valvita cooks rice and beans,
we take turns cuddling her new grandson.
Meanwhile, Shirley takes instant photographs of every family in
      Patio Grande.
"*Muchísimas gracias, señora*," a man says. "If more of us die,
the world will not be able to forget us!"
We do not dare spit out the boiled bananas, Valvita's special treat.

In the event of an attack, Ed advised us yesterday,
sink down in the direction of the shots.
He is 70 years old and wears a bow-tie even in the jungle.
The rest of us do not hear the shot, but he sinks down.
He sinks down, and a hammock begins to swing slowly,
      inevitably, into the afternoon.

PALE MOON OVER KIGALI

Like everyone else, I've been riveted to Rwanda,
to the dead bodies of Tutsis floating downriver as if toward me—
black bodies bleaching strangely white in the relentless sun.

Here, it's April, dogwood season, paroxysms of blossoms in our
    front yard.
I'm pregnant for the first time ever.
Whenever I look in the mirror, I see veins flowing like swollen
    rivers to my breasts.
I am just beginning to feel a body moving inside my body.
The movement is fluttery like a breeze.

"Chaos: A Vector Analysis" is a friend's reading
of the ultrasound pictures I hang on the refrigerator.
I'll admit there's something inchoate about them, but I can
    recognize
a shadowy body, even if I need the white arrows
to identify the parts: head, nose, chin; hand, wrist, arm; heel,
    foot, toes.

My belly rises slowly like the pale moon over Kigali.
In May, I hear a telephone interview with an American
    missionary who survived the massacres.
She says, my neighbors were poor—they didn't use guns, they
    used machetes.
Outside her compound, she sees the hacked-up bodies.

I am terrified of birth.
I am terrified of death.
In the bathroom one morning, I convince myself I have had a
    miscarriage.
I am embarrassed when I discover that the blood clots are the
    red peppers I had for dinner.

By July, the Hutu refugees have begun pouring into Goma.
I watch them dying like flies from cholera and being wrapped in
    straw mats by the roadside.

An old man crawls on top of the dead bodies
French soldiers are already bulldozing into mass graves.
He refuses to move.
He believes it is foolish to waste the effort.

"Do you think the Tutsis will kill you?"
A clubby reporter interviews
a hollow-eyed Hutu boy
who has lost his mother, father, and six brothers and sisters
on the road to Goma. "Did you ever *know* a Tutsi?"
The boy answers out of a deep cave:
"My mother. My mother was a Tutsi."

In the seventh month, I begin to lumber, like a cow in a thicket.
When I get up to go to the bathroom in the middle of the night,
I hear sorrowful mooing I'm afraid is my own.

My husband is worried
about the diagnosis of gestational diabetes.
He sighs when he puts his arms around my big belly,
as if he's convinced it will do no good
to measure the circumference of the troubled world.

Every Monday, we hear our baby's heartbeat.
We're not afraid to confess how much hearing it awes us.
It's as if we hear drops of the most incredible, most viscous
            sweetness
dripping, dripping, dripping from a secret faucet we ourselves
            have turned on at the center of the universe.
There's nothing demure about this sweetness,
which rolls in like thunder when the nurse turns on the fetal
            monitor.

On the late news, I hear that refugees flooding out of Rwanda
            are being trampled to death.
All night, my baby keeps me awake with its strong kicking.

BULLETIN BOARD

When I discovered that all the postcards of black authors had
      been defaced,
I heard my voice crackling, as in a radio transmission from outer space.
The world was waiting for me to deliver an important message,
      but I was an astronaut, not a poet.
The best I could do was paraphrase someone else's efforts:
"That's one small step back for a man, one giant leap backward
      for mankind."
Through the window of my classroom, I could see the Columbia
      Point Housing Project
rising up in front of me like a lost planet.
Asphalt and cinder blocks were its most distinctive surface features.
I remembered the alien boy who had landed from there in my classroom.
When I called on him to read, he had inched his long black
      finger across the page,
sounding out each syllable as if he were in second grade.
By the end of a week, he had given up on other universes.
I imagined him back in the projects, leaping up for a jump shot
      into a basketball hoop without a net.
He had been recruited as a basketball star. I heard the basketball
      bouncing, bouncing, bouncing.
"Don't blame us, we didn't do it," my students insisted. "Don't
      blame us, don't blame us."
I studied, below me, the small white dot of each worried face.
Earth, with its oceans and rivers, mountains and forests, kept
      swirling and swirling.
I said, "Léopold Sédar Senghor was the President of Senegal as
      well as a poet.
He was born in Joal, a fishing village where I once ate tortoise
      meat and rice out of a bowl with my hands.
At low tide, we waded out to a shell island, where the granaries,
      on stilts above the water,
looked like old people with thick torsoes and skinny legs.
At dawn, the fishermen, in flowing robes, set out to sea in their
      tiny pirogues . . . "
I started with Senghor because his face had suffered the biggest gash.
One by one, I held up the defaced postcards, praying and praying
      over the face of the earth.

III

NIGHT OWL

From you, I inherited this starry flesh.
The night is young, the night is young—my voice is your voice in
      endless mimicry.

Thirty years ago, sleepless and hungry for quarry, I caught you
      drinking milk of magnesia,
staring into the kitchen sink as into a deep well.
Father, if you had jumped in, I would have had to follow.

How many times I space-walked toward you across the pock-
      marked moonfloor,
triumphant in my pajamas before the less courageous world.
Gravity was your unfailing argument: *just what, young lady, do*
      you think you're doing up?

Tonight, bills unopened, heart too in arrears,
I remember how the muscles in your face relaxed.
To ease your cares, it was enough for you to know that I didn't
      have any.
And so we discussed kindergarten, the moon and the stars.

MOONSCAPE, THE GULF CRISIS

1.

I am afraid I have lost my husband
to the faceless dead.
He refuses to turn off the television.
He prays by osmosis:
world without end . . .

2.

I too have terrorized
the innocent. One Friday afternoon,
in my first year of teaching
at an all-boys school, I might as well
have been shouting, *You want me*
to tear out your love machines? You want me
to pluck out your eyeballs? You want me to send you home
in body bags? instead of teaching Shakespeare.
Two or three sneering faces
had provoked me to sacrifice the others.
When the bell rang, my face
rose small and wan,
the moon over the battlefield.

3.

Oh mother, until I whisper, "Good night, moon. Good night,
stars in the sky," out the shadowy window,
I am incapable of sleep.

Last summer, the doctors broke my nephew's arm
trying to extricate him from the womb.
I did not fly home
to say good bye to him in his tiny coffin,
nor watch them bury him
beside my father:
Colin William, stillborn.

4.

Oh father, moon mirror, waxing and waning
in the night sky over Green Harbor!

The night of your funeral, I howled
and howled at the moon
like a ferocious dog.
I swore my teeth of grief would sink
into everything alive.

Beware of dog. Beware of moon.

Once, father, you sent me a postcard
from your hotel room.
On one side, a white-blooming tree
like a lacy doily.
On the other, *The Legend of the Flowering Dogwood.*
I was just learning to read.
I forget, now, how the dogwood got its name.
Did ferocity flower?

Oh moon, take pity.
Oh moon, take pity.

I do not know whether I would ever
have tasted joy again
if Ellen had not invited
the Down's-syndrome children into our home.
That was two years after your funeral.
The twelve years since then have been a dogwood dream,
stripped bare again
every winter, but blossoming,
beyond grief, in springtime.

I will never forget
those bright faces orbiting around us.

It was as if those children,
who, in other centuries, had been locked up
in cellars like ferocious dogs,
took our hands and led us out
of the deepest darkness.
Your widow.
Your seven children.

At the end of the day, we played baseball.
When, at long last, she hit the ball,
one girl insisted on running
to third base instead of first
because she wanted to kiss
the third baseman, your son John.
That was how gentle we had become.

5.

Once, in the sweet relapse
after lovemaking, a man stuttering in awe
of what he thought we had proven
—*joy is a kind of defenselessness*—
told me, at long last, that his mother was not dead
as he had allowed me to think
but dead to him.

All night, I cradled him in my arms
like the *Stabat Mater*. Heavy, heavy
his sleeping body. Heavy the silence in which
I could not sleep. In the grotto
of my grieving face, I discovered
a virgin spring.

6.

In which
burning book
did I read the story?

An old Jew, himself
the night's detritus, coughing blood,
crawled through pools of excrement
to chant "praise God" in moonlight.

The witnesses, eyes watery
as thin broth, rose disbelieving
out of their bunks to accuse him:
"Do you want us
to die tomorrow,
oh skeleton of skeletons?
Sleep is our only hope."

But the human voice
makes such exquisite music.
They had forgotten.
They crowded together at the door
of the bunkhouse, the thin bones of their arms
pressed together like wings.

Lift up your hearts!

And so they flew to their deaths like moths.

7.

Last night, after singing
O come, o come, Emanuel
to the accompaniment of cello (hope is a deep,
dark, resonant virtue),
I stepped out of church
just in time to watch two cars crash.

"How could you have been so morbid?"
a friend asks me
when I tell her over the telephone
that I stood there for two hours while a police crew
excavated the bodies.

I tell her I didn't know that the dead were dead.

It is the third week of Advent, late
afternoon. I stare
out the living room window
at the pale orb of the moon.

8.

The soldiers on television
are the same age as my students.
I assign a weekly
composition: "How are *your* hearts
'lonely hunters'?"

Again, they try to answer by refusing
loneliness, but this time
the desert in the background forces
a topic sentence on them:
the enemy is not fully human,
so it is all right to kill him.

9.

Mame Diaga, my Muslim
grandfather, must be dead now
in Senegal, my adopted country.
I loved him with my whole heart,
and yet I scared him, one night,
nearly out of his wits.

I only wanted to take him to a movie
for the first time
in his life. Of course, I knew better
than to subject him to the French skin flicks.
Star Wars was showing, and I thought
—because he had two wives himself—
he might enjoy the intergalactic love story
of Luke Skywalker and Princess Leia.

In the battle scenes, he covered his ears.
He had never before
caught a glimpse of a spaceship,
not even in cartoons.
In boyhood a daring warrior, he had never dreamed
of firing anything like a laser gun.
When he looked out
every night at the scintillating universe
(in Fatick, the moon and the stars
were always visible because so few people had electricity),
he had never imagined
evil planets.

The force be with you!

On the way home, he chose to keep silent
about his great grief.

He said good night in the same
tone of voice in which he had once told me
that a woman in the next village
had drowned herself
in a well. The next thing I knew,
he had unrolled his prayer mat in my courtyard.
I felt guilty and stupid.
I was almost grateful
I couldn't sleep because he prayed out loud.
"Allah" was the only word I could understand.

10.

Oh mother of the dark ravine,
Oh tortured and bleeding, never to be seen again,
Oh full moon, oh full moon, oh full moon.

Again, something terrible
has happened.

This time, I don't get a phone call.

Again, the worst has happened.
I walk into a room. I do not have to look
into anyone's eyes.

We have bombed Baghdad.
Thousands will die.

Over and over, I hear the thud
of my father's body.
His is the only death I know concretely.

Other deaths are still abstract.

Suzanne's, for example.
She sang the *Ave Maria* at my father's funeral.
Now she has cancer.
If she must die so young,
I want her, at the very least, to die in peace.

But now bombs are dropping.

I read that the children of Kuwait have regressed
since the occupation.
Some are wetting their beds again.
Some have forgotten
all the words in their vocabularies.
Now, the children of Iraq will start forgetting.

Blessed are the peacemakers,
for they shall be called children of God.

One Kuwaiti mother,
afraid her children had suffered permanent
psychological damage, took them
up to the roof one night
(in daylight, someone could have seen her
and accused her of insurrection)
and taught them how to shout again.

At first, the children
could only whisper: *Allahu Akbar.*
It took patient coaching
to get them to increase in volume, a little
at a time, until finally
they shouted from the rooftops: *Allahu Akbar! Allahu Akbar!*

God is great, greater, greatest.
Greater than what?
Fear.

Suzanne's lungs are collapsing.
It is too late to tell her
that she sounded like an angel at my father's funeral.
The angel said, "Be not afraid."

For months, I have been afraid again.

Every night, at the same time,
my husband gets restless and calls me from the porch:
"Come look at the moon."

I wipe my hands
on a dirty dish towel, and come.

There is nothing to do in those moments
but hold each other
until, as if betrayed
by tenderness, we're almost sobbing.

There is nothing to do in those moments
but hold each other and shine.

WHATEVER CREPT AWAY

It was the night of the blessing of the fleet,
and I wanted to write you a poem as fine as your shoulders,
lifting anchor and hauling traps. I tried hard for a month,
but it was your fault, your shoulders kept interfering.
A year later, it is time for conching again, and we watch
the horseshoe crabs lob up on the beach to lay their eggs.

"What would I do," you say, "if the Portuguese
didn't eat conchs? I'd be even poorer." But today,
we are poor, we don't eat anything ourselves. We vanish
for the first time into poor house, poor boat, poor light, poor luck.

I tell you about the night I woke up mourning
crabs: I was nine years old and had spent my day collecting a dozen
       baby crabs. By supper time, the ice cube tray
       on the porch was empty. En route to the ocean, my crabs
       perished by catching their pincers in the slats.
You laugh, and I think, 'here
is another being whose legs I have counted in sleep.'

Later, the conch I plop into the pot looks like an ear, we have
ears on our laps for the last time. The Portuguese druggist
sent in an order for twenty-five pounds. Someone's daughter
must be getting married. We watch the water suck out
the grey conch flesh. I'm not a bride, I want them alive still,
our wrestled creatures. You hand me the shell with the widest
open mouth—its nerves gone, its stars eaten.

Last summer, when we took in the big fish, we let the captain
steer while we climbed up to the sighting deck.
It was only ten in the morning, and you were done working.
There was a space in the wind that loved us, loved
the lapping water. We counted the flitting candles of the sailboats.
Everything else was so tiny, from that roof, following home.

WORLD SERIES

We are humbled by the vehemence of the earth,
which must finally have taken our sins to heart.
In this emergency, we begin to understand seismology, life and
   death colliding like tectonic plates.
Apocalypse is a radio broadcast: *I am standing outside a building
   in which human beings are burning alive.*
Last weekend, in the mountains, quaking aspens were a
   prefiguration.
It is still October, but we no longer whisper *beloved autumn flame.*

Nor are telephones immortal creatures.
In the first of thousands of aftershocks, we tremble into their ears:
"Mother, father, sister, brother—I was true to my habits. I am
   therefore alive.
I was not driving on the freeway when it collapsed—a foolishness
of which you accused me because today is no different from any
   other
in only *one* respect: you insist on loving me to absurdity."

In the blackout, it is back to Genesis. Television undreamed of,
World Series eclipsed by earthquake, sacrifice upon the face of
   the deep.
"Let there be light, let there be light," cries out an old man
twenty years too fragile for the crowds at the ballpark, too senile
   to remember
that baseball was not invented until the seventh day
when God rested because the din of life, not death, gave Him a
   headache.

Somehow, in a nightmare's dictionary, baseball becomes a
   synonym for faith, hope and charity.
Perhaps the catcher in his death mask strikes awe in us. Simple-
   minded in the aftermath,
perhaps we all grope toward the same analogy: the earth is to a
   baseball as the hand of God
is to *my* hand. Or perhaps, when the earth opened up to
   swallow us,

we wore a baseball diamond on one finger like a jewel from the
          bowels of the earth to help us pray:
Compel us, like black coal, to scintillation, in this twenty-second eon.

The dead begin to appear to us as baseball stars in pearl grey
          uniforms.
The moon is a shadowy baseball we ask them to autograph.
The host on the radio talk show is unequivocal—*the World
          Series must be cancelled*—
but we do not defer to him. We rise for the National Anthem.
We sing sweetly, in spite of ourselves, like child prodigies
          shipwrecked on a desert island:
Oh say can you see, oh say can you see the world is not ending, the
          world is beginning again.

IV

PEACEABLE KINGDOM

Our son is born naked as Adam.
We hold him for a minute in a thick, thick towel.
His hair is matted and bloody.
We speak to him awkwardly because he is a stranger, and besides,
　　　we don't want the doctor and nurses to overhear.
He stops howling and contemplates us warily.
Thus does he begin to discover his own multifariousness.

Once, after hiking all day through black filigree of dessicated
　　　maidenhair fern
in a summer so dry the coyotes ventured down from the hills to
　　　catch the drippings from hoses,
I came, at dusk, to a group of hikers taking cover behind prickly poppy.
They pointed to an island of green grass where deer were feeding.
We watched the deer nuzzle, cavort and loll around.
We watched their shadows ripen slowly like peaches on a
　　　kitchen table.
Over and over, we said, 'what exquisite creatures.'
In the year after our son is born, our lives are the fertile island
　　　at which everyone is pointing.
We are the exquisite creatures.

Thank God for the dove boy who coos after every feeding.
Thank God for the frog boy who kicks to both sides of his bath at once.
Thank God for the pig boy who finally turns over after grunting
　　　for twenty minutes.

Soon our son wriggles across the living room floor.
He evolves to creeping, then crawling.
We race after him, exaggerating the pounding of our feet.
He loves being a small animal pursued by two big animals at
　　　peril of his life.

He dares to look over his shoulder in the adrenaline rush.
He is determined to make it to the storm door ahead of us to
　　　press the fossil print of his lips into the glass.
When he reaches the door, he pounds it in triumph.

Hooray, hooray.
Months go by.
Along the ocean, we stare at our son's first footprints in the sand, so
    beautiful and primitive.
I keep struggling to remember something.
One day it whizzes by me like an arrow out of the trees.
I was at a wedding reception.
I thought I heard an animal in the bushes.
A man with no legs and only one arm bounded toward me on
    his one arm.
He was the bride's uncle.
He had been in a terrible accident in boot camp at age 18.
He shook my hand.
He introduced me to his wife and three children.
Motion is joy.

Thank God for the rooster boy who crows with delight
    whenever he is hiding and we find him.
Thank God for the chimpanzee boy who doesn't know his own
    strength, who hurls himself gleefully at us.
Thank God for the sea-lion boy who bellows on the beach of
    his bedtime.

Spring arrives.
The quince and the forsythia are beautiful even through dirty windows.
We spend an entire morning washing the first-floor windows,
    inside and outside,
in preparation for the luminous dogwood.
Dirty water runs to the ground in little streams.
That afternoon, our son falls sick.
We take turns holding him as he vomits.
We take turns doing his laundry.

He's too sick to eat.
He's too sick to drink.
After every siege of his body, he smiles at us weakly.
I remember being terrified when a student's father called to tell
    me his son had committed suicide.

Would I agree to answer a few questions about his son's poetry?
I would, although I was afraid that doing so would be like pinning
        blossoms back on a stricken tree.
When he saw me enter the lobby of his son's dormitory, the
        father struggled up out of the couch.
His lips brushed his wife's lips before he extended his hand.
The kiss was almost perfunctory.
It couldn't have been further from the famous kiss in the
        pounding surf in *From Here to Eternity*.
Yet it seemed more eternal.
A creature's habits can be excruciatingly beautiful.
Our son smiles at us again and again out of his ghost body.
We stay inside with him until he gets better.
Afterwards, we rake up the rotting pink tulip-poplar blossoms
        that have fallen while he was sick.
The rake feels good in our hands, like bony fingers scraping the ground.
The dogwood is still in bloom.

Now our son scrambles down from our laps, hanging on to the
        edges of our chairs until gravity assists him to the grass.
Now he stands giddily alone for thirty seconds.
Now he takes one step, two steps, before throwing himself into
        our arms in front of ripening tomato vines.

Yesterday, our son spilled the glass of water on our bedside table.
When he was just born and couldn't see well, he used to root
        out my breasts with his tiny mouth.
Watching him was like watching my own hand reach out in the
        dark for something I know is there, for example, the
        glass of water on our bedside table.
We always reach for it after making love,
as if to substantiate the ordinary world.
The glass always feels cold and slightly wet in our hands, like an
        apple with dew on it.
We bring it to our lips.
We drink, drink.
Soon the glass is empty because we are full.
Then we fall easily asleep.

BLACK POEM FOR A WHITE EGRET

I stare into every night as into a deep lake.
My son wakes up.
I dive in the direction of his cries.

Every morning, motherhood settles over me
like a beautiful fog.
My son is always at my breast.
I can make out my husband a few feet away.
Everyone else is indistinct, although I can hear their voices.

My son is two months old.
Over years and years, the idea of him, like a white egret
stalking me with its beauty.
I'd stare into the burnt grass on a summer day.
Suddenly I'd hear a slight stirring,
then I'd see the exquisite creature.
From a distance, I could almost pluck its legs
like harpstrings.

My son sleeps in the early afternoon.
I stand by his crib.
I listen to the gentle lapping of his breathing.
I do not remember what the night has eroded away.
By late afternoon, my eyes feel like pebbles.
Worries escape from me
in concentric circles,
as if I've thrown my eyes into the water.

I blame everything on hormones.
I'm afraid of what I'm shedding.
I know it's not light.

Today I entrust my son to a stranger,
the eye-doctor's secretary,
who tells me over the phone
that she'll take care of him while I get an eye exam.

There's so much filth in this world.
This is what the man with the patch over his eye
says in the eye-doctor's waiting room
about the woman on the news
who strapped her two little boys
into their carseats,
then pushed the car into a lake.

I'll bet *he* has never watched
flakes of instant baby cereal fly off
the sharp knife of each day
like fish scales.

I want two kids to tug all day on the line of his patience.
I want them to wriggle and wriggle until he catches them.
I want him to feel triumphant.
I want them to get sick and to go limp slowly like fish in a bucket.
I want him to realize, too late, that they're going limp.
He had intended to release them, eventually, in a big-hearted gesture,
into the rushing waters of their lives.
I want him to be afraid they'll die on him.
I want them both to begin spewing forth at once.
I want him to have to decide whose hot head to hold.
I want him to have to sit there in all the effluvia
trying not to confuse motherhood
with a pond lily.

Nobody answers the man.
Everybody sees two boys.
Everybody sees the water rising, rising, rising
around them
like a slow elevator
into the blue sky.

Even the man who thinks their mother is human litter
would do anything to save them.

I imagine the murderer driving home from a day at the lake last
        summer.
She sees her kids' heads bobbing up and down, but her heart
        doesn't start to plummet.
She's just glancing into the rear-view mirror. The kids are already
        out of the water.
They're so pooped from overworking at the dog-paddle that
        they fall asleep before she can even pull out of the lot.
A few moments after she comes to a final stop, they cry out like
        loons
in the raspy beauty of discovering something huge and strange
        and raw inside them.
At first, she can't get them out of their carseats because their
        legs are caught.
She has to disentangle them from their seatbelts as from reeds or
        plankton.
After putting them to bed, she stands in the dark hallway
        outside their bedroom.
She stands very still, until she is the lake, and their breathing
        carries like familiar music across her.

Staying awake
to feed my son in the early morning
is like driving across
an incredibly long bridge.
I could succumb to tunnel vision.
I could crash our lives
into the black railings that converge
on the other side
in a flash of light.
Sometimes I fall asleep for a second.
I wake up feeling guilty.
My son could have plunged to his death.
I am glad he is alive,
but my gladness
is too close to panic.

Who knows how many miles
lie ahead of us.
The view is beautiful but terrifying.
I have no choice but to keep driving
with my heart in my mouth.

My son is two months old.
I hold him and hold him and hold him.
I never want to let him go.

EASTER VIGIL

I remember being a young girl in a pink coat at the Easter Vigil.
The only seats left were in the rear of the church with all the grey
    bodies.
They smelled like smoke.
During the long readings, they hacked and hacked so that I
    couldn't hear anything.
They half sat and half knelt when they were supposed to kneel,
    making their backs look like inclined planes.
They were mostly longshoremen.
In school, we had memorized the line, *I must down to the seas
    again, the lonely sea and the sky.*
I did not think these men went down to the docks to breathe in
    the lonely sea and the sky.
In summer, the door to the corner bar was open, and I could see
    them drinking inside.
I could smell the beer they had spilled on the floor.
I imagined their shoes sticking to the kitchen linoleum when they
    got home, as if their wives had spilled honey.
But their wives were bitter as gall.
I knew because I heard them shouting sometimes at three in the
    morning.
The service was long.
The grey bodies around me shifted uneasily in their seats.
A few genuflected sloppily on their way outside.
Many times I had seen them leaning grimly against the churchyard
    wall, as if they were about to be shot by a firing squad
    instead of about to light up their cigarettes.
When it came time to extinguish our candles, I was tempted to disobey.
I obeyed anyway.
I was attracted, too, to the darkness in my life.

Sometimes, in taking stock of my life, I have felt like the blind
    man in the parable trying to describe an elephant.
I touch its legs and say it's like a tree trunk.
I touch its trunk and say, no, it's more like a snake.
I touch its sides and say no, no, it's like a wall.
I can't fathom the huge grey bulk of it.

Once, I drove downtown with my father in a big Chrysler that
was running on empty.

It was a Sunday, grey and raw.

The sidewalks were deserted.

We pulled into a seedy gas station because it was the only one open.

It must have been close to Easter. There were lilies lining the
pumps. Exhaust was turning them dingy.

As we pulled out, my father turned to me and asked, "If I die,
will you go to my funeral?"

I knew he wasn't joking because his voice sounded small and choked.

A man we knew had just left his family. He had given no reason. He
had just disappeared suddenly, as if he had been kidnapped
by aliens.

I said yes to my father in a tiny voice.

I understood that my father's elephant could trample us all to death.

"I never loved him, not even on the day I married him," a friend
tells me in the wake of her divorce.

I tell her I don't believe her, but she insists.

When my husband and I went to talk to the priest before we got
married, he asked us, "who will your role models be in
this difficult vocation?"

I said "my mother and father."

My husband said, "I don't know. Nobody in my family has ever
stayed married."

I wished that we could turn history inside out as easily as a sock.

In the hour before our son was born, my husband stood quietly
by me in the dim birthing room.

He is a tall, thin man.

His complexion was eerily waxy.

He was the Easter candle I would light, when the time came, out
of the flaming bowl of my body.

Push, the doctor said, *push, push.*

My mother could have buried herself in a tomb when my father died.
She could have dabbed herself with spirits of camphor and rolled
        towels under her doors like my grandmother did to keep
        the noises of children out.
"She died with him," the mourners said at my grandmother's
        funeral, twenty five years after my grandfather's.

Instead my mother told me
to turn slowly, slowly, on the dining room table so that she
        could pin up the hem of my Easter suit.
She had pins in her mouth.
I imagined I was rotating on the axis of the earth.
My geography teacher had drawn it on the board although it
        was really invisible.
All night, my mother hemmed and sewed on buttons.
The next morning, she hid behind the front door whenever she
        opened it so that passers-by would not see she was still
        in her bathrobe.
Easter was wintry.
Other children were already shivering on their way to the
        Children's Mass.
She wanted us to shiver too.
We were like crocuses pushing up out of the cold earth.
We said deadness is an illusion.
Always there is new life buried within.

I didn't tell my mother I was pregnant until the end of the
        fourth month
because I was terrified of her joy.

Alleluia, alleluia.
Our son burst forth.

It was difficult to sit still in a hard pew during the long haul of
        the Easter Vigil.
The men who had absconded to the churchyard eventually
        shuffled back inside.

Beads of rain dangled from the wool of their overcoats as from
    spiderwebs.
They never took off their overcoats—what were they hiding
    underneath?
By this time, all the lights in the church were off.
Staring into the grainy dark was like staring into the snow on a
    late-night TV screen.
Suddenly, there was a stirring at the rear of the church.
Like a bat, our attention swooped down on the priest in his
    vestments.

Out of the grey body beside me, I heard a moan.
It reminded me of the moan of the sea on a stormy night.

The priest lit the Easter candle.

I vowed to sail all over the world, announcing in every dark port,
"She really loved him. She didn't mean it when she said she didn't."

Today is an ordinary day.
I wait for my son to wake up from his nap.
I wait for my husband to come home.
I take the dark socks out of the dryer.
I roll them up in pairs.
I pile them up on the laundry table like loaves of brown bread.
Inside each one rises the yeast of our lives.

ANN NEELON *is a native of Boston and a graduate of the MFA
Program at the University of Massachusetts, Amherst, and of Holy Cross
College. She has been a Peace Corps Volunteer in West Africa, as well as
a Stegner Fellow and Jones Lecturer at Stanford University.*

Her poems and translations have appeared in American Poetry Review,
Gettysburg Review, Ironwood, Calyx, Pequod, Poetry East,
Manoa, Michigan Quarterly Review, *and other magazines. She lives
with her husband and son in western Kentucky, where she is Assistant
Professor of English at Murray State University.*

ANHINGA PRIZE FOR POETRY

Selection	Year / Judge
Ann Neelon *Easter Vigil*	1995 Joy Harjo
Frank X. Gaspar *Mass for the Grace of a Happy Death*	1994 Joy Harjo
Janet Holmes *The Physicist at the Mall*	1993 Joy Harjo
Earl S. Braggs *Hat Dancer Blue*	1992 Marvin Bell
Jean Monahan *Hands*	1991 Donald Hall
Nick Bozanic *The Long Drive Home*	1989 Judith Hemschemeyer
Julianne Seeman *Enough Light to See*	1988 Charles Wright
Will Wells *Conversing with the Light*	1987 Henry Taylor
Robert Levy *The Whistle Maker*	1986 Robin Skelton
Judith Kitchen *Perennials*	1985 Hayden Carruth
Sherry Rind *The Hawk in the Backyard*	1984 Louis Simpson
Ricardo Pau-Llosa *Sorting Metaphors*	1983 William Stafford

RECENT BOOKS FROM ANHINGA

Van K. Brock — *Unspeakable Strangers*
Poems about the Holocaust

Long, Wallace, Campbell, eds. — *Isle of Flowers: Poems by*
Florida's Individual Artist Fellows

P.V. LeForge — *The Secret Life of Moles*

Gary Corseri — *Random Descent*

Ryals and Decker, eds. — *North of Wakulla:*
An Anhinga Anthology

FORTHCOMING FROM ANHINGA

Robert Dana — *Hello, Stranger*

Michael Mott — *Selected Poems*

Nick Bozanic — *This Once*

Earl S. Braggs — *Walking Back from Woodstock*